How To Triumph Over Sickness

by
Norvel Hayes

HARRISON HOUSE
Tulsa, Oklahoma

Unless otherwise indicated,
all Scripture quotations are taken from
the *King James Version* of the Bible.

How To Triumph Over Sickness
ISBN 0-89274-702-1
Copyright © 1982 by Norvel Hayes
P. O. Box 1379
Cleveland, Tennessee 37311
(Formerly *Your Faith Can Heal You*, ISBN 0-89274-273-9)

Published by Harrison House, Inc.
P. O. Box 35035
Tulsa, Oklahoma 74153

Contents

Foreword

About the Author:

The author of this book is a Christian business layman who has an unusual burden and deep dedication to God's work. He is a member of the Full Gospel Business Men's Fellowship and is one of their international directors.

He makes no pretense of literary style, but teaches the Word in its simplicity so that people of all ages and classes can understand and comprehend its messages. He is a man of daring and dynamic faith—a faith that is not often exhibited in a layman—and he is perhaps one of the busiest Christian laymen in America. He flies from coast to coast, anywhere that his ministry of prayer and faith is needed, and he has ministered overseas.

Not only is he a very successful businessman, but by applying the same principles of faith to his ministry as he does to his businesses, he has gained much repute and respect both in the religious and the business world.

His style is unique, and at times may seem a bit redundant. Nevertheless, it is penetrating to the mind in such a way that one does not soon forget his teachings.

His purpose in writing this book is to help Christians of all denominations to be able to read some of the same messages which he presents in his seminars, and as they read them, he hopes that they will realize what they actually are in Christ, through His Word, and through His great plan of redemption. The constant theme of this book is the challenge to believers to act upon their faith.

It is with great pleasure that we present *Your Faith Can Heal You.*

REV. H. M. M. KEELE

1

Your Faith

I want to talk to you about your faith. If you are dying from a disease or affliction that has come upon your body, I want to tell you that you don't have to die. Death is an enemy of God and God doesn't put disease or any kind of affliction upon the human race. No sickness or disease comes from heaven because there is not any there. God is the Boss in heaven and He does not create disease of any kind, or any kind of affliction to put on and in human bodies to cause heartaches.

People spend thousands of dollars to try to find a healing and a cure. The enemy of God, the devil, is the cause of all sickness and all diseases, but it is God's will to heal everybody and it is God's will to heal you because, you see, God's Word is God's will.

The Bible is God's perfect will for the human race to live by, but if you don't know what the Bible says, then you can't live by it. You tend to live by suggestions that come to you through the power of the devil. He will always suggest to you to rely on religion, your own way, doing what you want to do, and will keep your physical being from serving God. He will also keep you away from the church that believes what the

Bible says. A great trick which the devil has played on the human race is to get people involved with a church that doesn't believe in healing of the body.

Healing is in the atonement, as well as salvation, but Satan will try to get you to disbelieve it, or to overlook it, or to ignore it because he wants to not only destroy you mentally and spiritually, but he wants you to also doubt that God really cares about your physical well-being as well.

This way, he has right-of-way or free access to attack your body because your faith is not in the healing power of the Lord Jesus Christ.

The enemy will keep you from that which the Bible actually teaches. You see, the Bible is the Truth, and there is no other truth on the face of the earth for you or anybody else.

I want you to notice in the Book of John in the New Testament, chapter 8, verse 32: Jesus said, "And ye shall know the truth, and the truth shall make you free." Everybody, anybody who knows the truth—the truth shall make you free. Jesus does not tell lies. Jesus said, *"And ye shall know the truth, and the truth shall make you free."*

It is not just the truth that makes you free, it is *knowing the truth* that makes you free! You see, even though He took your infirmities and bore your sicknesses, just as He bore your sins, if you don't know that, you won't be made free. The Word is the Truth!

The New Testament is the covenant under which you are living. Testament means covenant. A covenant is an agreement between two or more parties. It is your responsibility to find out what is in the New Testament because everything written therein is for your benefit. It is for you because God is no respecter of persons. What Jesus did for others, He will also do for you.

Notice in the Book of Galatians, chapter 5, verse 1, the Apostle Paul says, "Stand fast therefore in the liberty wherewith Christ hath made us free, and be not entangled again with the yoke of bondage."

I ask you to stand fast, or steadily, in the promises of the verses of Scriptures that you read from the Bible, and your body will be made whole if you will stand without wavering (vacillating or doubting).

Don't get entangled with people's thoughts or the religious ideas of those who do not believe what the Bible says about the healing of the body. This is a snare to entangle you.

Your faith can heal you, but your faith must be based upon what is written and not on the sentiments and opinions of man. It must be based entirely on what is written.

Now read the thirty-sixth verse of the Book of John, chapter 8: "If the Son therefore shall make you free, ye shall be free indeed." The Son will make you free because you believe His Word. Now the truth is this: *You are already healed because the Word says you are healed!* Our Lord took our infirmities, our sicknesses, and our diseases upon Himself. First Peter 2:24 declares, "Who his own self bare our sins in his own body on the tree, that we, being dead to sins, should live unto righteousness: by whose stripes ye were healed."

Then if you were healed, you don't have to be healed sometime in the future, because "you were healed" is past tense and the Word says *you are already healed*. All you have to do is accept it! Accept what? Accept what the Word says about healing for your body, about what He says about God's power going through your body so you can be free, about complete deliverance from the oppression of the devil. Claim God's Word. Your faith can heal you!

A Woman's Faith Heals Her

In a certain city one time I prayed for a woman who had just about reached the end of the road for her life. Jesus led her to me for help, but I felt that I should have the assistance of another man, who was a minister. As I was going to call him, suddenly the Spirit of God came upon me and as I stopped in the hallway, the Word of the Lord came unto me saying, *You don't need that minister; you need Me,* and I said, "All right, Jesus, I know that, so I will go back and pray for the woman myself." I went back out and fell to my knees beside her, in the middle of the floor, and began to pray. I had only been praying about two minutes when suddenly the power of God came upon her and hit her with such force that she rose to her feet and began to scream, rejoice, and shout. Then she began to dance in the Spirit under the mighty power of God for several minutes. (The Old Testament records that King David danced under the mighty power of God before the ark of the covenant, and his wife became cursed by the

Lord and was childless all the days of her life because she made fun of this sacred manifestation of God's power upon King David.) As she danced under the power of God, she was healed in a supernatural way, in body, mind, and spirit.

When Jesus uses you to help pray someone else from the powers of darkness or sickness and to bring him into His marvelous light, that person whom Jesus' power came through usually has a deep feeling of gratitude for you. Even though he realizes that Jesus is the One who did the healing, it is only natural that he has a high regard for the "vessel" whom God uses. For that reason, some years later when this woman became seriously ill, I was called to pray for her. She had been in the hospital for more than two weeks. Friends and ministers came by and prayed for her and nothing happened. She said her husband, "When Norvel Hayes comes, I will be healed."

As soon as I arrived in town her husband came to me and asked me to come to the hospital. He stated, "She thinks that she will be healed when you come to the hospital."

I said, "Well, if that is what she believes, she surely will, but it will be because she trusts in Jesus, and not in me."

When we walked into her room and looked at her, I said, "Oh, thank God for your healing!" Then, because we as believers have the authority, I put my hand on her head and began to pray. I commanded the devil to take his hand and power off of her body, and I said, "In the name of Jesus Christ, I bind your power, Satan, and I command you to leave this body alone. I'm not asking you; I am commanding you! Go from her body now in the name of Jesus Christ." Then I claimed the healing power of the Lord Jesus Christ and God's healing power began to flow in her body and within five minutes she was completely healed.

When I first came into the room, she was nearly dead, but God's mighty power began to flow through her body and she lay on the bed quivering under His power as if she had been shot with a gun.

They had put large weights on her feet and I told her husband, "If she were my wife, I'd take those weights off her feet and carry her out of this hospital because the hospital staff will put doubt back in her; they won't mean to, but they will."

She soon checked out of the hospital and was well. After some time the symptoms began to try to come back, but she didn't resist the enemy as she should have in the name of the Lord, so she decided to go to a service in another city, where a well-known and successful evangelist was conducting a salvation and healing service. While she was waiting in line, the Spirit of God came upon her and Jesus spake to her and said, *You are healed; you were healed in the hospital room that day*.

Immediately her faith began to rise up and she began to say, "Yes, I am healed! I am healed!" As she began to claim her healing out loud, the oppressing power of the devil left her, and it was thrilling to hear her testimony later of what Jesus had done for her. She was healed because she learned to use her faith.

God will also set your body, your mind, and your

spirit free by His mighty power, and He will do it on a permanent basis, according to your faith. Build your faith on His Word and trust Him now. There is no such thing as failing. Your faith can heal you!

2

Your Sick Body

Your sick body can be healed by your faith in God's Word. First of all, God wants your body to glorify His name. Has your body in the past been working for God? If not, and you have a disease in your body or if you are dying from a disease which the doctor says cannot be healed, I ask you to follow the advice of the Apostle Paul in the Book of Romans, chapter 12, verses 1 and 2. Paul says here:

I beseech you therefore, brethren, by the mercies of God, that ye present your bodies a living sacrifice, holy, acceptable unto God, which is your reasonable service. And be not conformed to [patterned after] this world: but be ye transformed [completely changed] by the renewing of your mind, that ye may prove what is that good, and acceptable, and perfect, will of God.

I want you to understand something right now so you will never forget it: It is up to you what you do with your body; it is not up to anybody else. You are a free, moral agent and you will either follow God's instructions and do something about presenting your body to God or nothing will ever be done about it, and you alone will reap the consequences.

This will help us to see the difference between the inward man and the outward man: Paul said, "I beseech you therefore, brethren," and he wasn't writing a letter to the world and the people who lived in the world— sinners, in other words—but he was writing to the saints, the Christians in Rome. He addressed the letter in Romans 1:7 "To all that be in Rome, beloved of God, called to be saints. . . ."

Of course, first of all, if you don't know Jesus as your personal Saviour, at this point you should tell Jesus that you are sincerely sorry for your sins and open up your heart and ask Him with your mouth to come in and live in your body and accept Him by faith and He will immediately change your spirit. Your spirit, in other words, will be reborn, and when you take your last breath when the time comes for you to go home, you will ascend out of your body and go to heaven to be with the Lord forever and ever.

In the meantime, God wants you to have a well, strong, healthy body. He wants every member of your body to walk in Him; God wants every member of your body to function normally; God doesn't want any affliction in your body and if you have any, God didn't put it there. His enemy, the power of darkness, the devil, put it there.

Jesus wants you to live an abundant life. He wants you to enjoy all the benefits which are provided for you in the New Testament. He wants you, your fellowship, your all. Your faith can heal you, but your faith must be founded in what God says in His Word.

His Word applies to all the beloved of God, called

to be saints, so Paul said, "I beseech you therefore, brethren, . . . that you present your bodies. . . ." *You do something with your body.* Do you understand me? You must do something with your body. Present it (bring it) to God for healing. If you don't do anything with it, nothing will ever be done with it.

In our church teachings, we have cluttered up some of this teaching until our minds are all confused and it is very difficult to get the real truth over to some people because of what they have been taught in the past. It is only what the Bible says that counts. Jesus said, "Ye shall know the truth, and the truth shall make you free" (John 8:32). You can't know the truth until you really read and study God's Word and take what He says at face value. Bible critics have tried to explain it away in an effort to destroy its authenticity, but you must be honest with God and with yourself and *know* the truth and *believe* the truth without questioning it and that truth will make you free!

I want you to notice something: He didn't say to present your body as a usual thing, or in the way that people usually interpret it (the Scriptures), but He wants us to present our bodies to Him for healing.

Our consecration and dedication services are often all out of line—not always according to the Scriptures. That is the reason they are not as effective as they ought to be. He didn't say for you to present your inward selves only to God, as some often interpret this Scripture, because if you are a child of God, you already belong to Him. You can't very well present to someone that which already belongs to him. He didn't say a word about dedicating yourselves in that sense because if you are already born again you are already His. You are that inward man that has become a new man in Christ.

Second Corinthians, chapter 5, verse 17 states, "Therefore if any man be in Christ, he is a new creature. . . ." What man is Paul talking about? This outward man? No, he is not. It couldn't be the outward man because he says that this man is a new creature. He is talking about presenting the physical body to God for healing, for strength, for power, and for health to better serve Christ.

We have missed this point in religious circles and religious teaching and preaching. People want folks to join the church; they want them merely to do better. Salvation is more than just joining the church and doing better; it is a new birth!

I never just tried to live right: I became born again, and I've been living right ever since because I was a new creature inside. When people are truly born again, their desires, appetites, ambitions, and affections change. They are new creatures in Christ. The devil has tried to defeat me by temptations, by lying to me, and by trying to deceive me. He has tried to bring habits back into my life, and tried to bring sin back into my life, but I would fall before the Lord and begin to pray and ask Jesus to help me and His mighty power never failed me.

Living a moral life is good and is to be commended, but it doesn't make you a Christian and it won't take you to heaven. Being born again by God's Spirit will take you to heaven. Mere resolutions become religion and religion isn't Christianity. Christianity is being

Christlike. Christianity is being born again, and receiving the gift of eternal life. When eternal life, which is the nature and the life of God, is imparted to your spirit, it changes you. It is easy then for you to read the Bible and it is easier for you to believe it. The devil does not give up easily. He will keep telling you differently and reminding you of things which you have been taught in the past, causing you to rely on what relatives or someone else told you rather than believing what God says. But if your spirit has been truly born again, it has the nature of God and there is something about that nature that doesn't like to accept anything and won't actually accept anything that isn't the Word of God. The spirit and the Word agree; therefore, anything which is contrary to God's Word will not be imbedded or relished by the truly born-again child of God who is a Bible believer. It is pertinent to our salvation that we measure all our past teachings by the Word of God. If they don't meet the true standards, then discard them!

Joy is one of the fruits of the Spirit. Your joy won't be full of the life of God until you make up your mind to accept God's Word just as it is. God's Word is truth and there is no other truth which can build your faith to the point where you can believe God. Then as you believe God's Word, your faith can heal you!

When you become born again by the Spirit of God, the inward man, your spirit, has been changed, but the outward man, your body, doesn't change when you accept Jesus as Saviour. The only thing that can change the condition of your body is when you accept Jesus Christ as your Healer. To do this, your faith has to be founded in the Scriptures that teach healing. Then God's healing power, by your faith, as you release it, will bring God's healing power into your body, and whatever part of your body is afflicted by disease or sickness, God's healing power will drive that sickness out if you stand steadfast in faith in God's Word and do not waver.

After the inward man becomes a new creature in Christ by the Spirit of God, he will have some trouble with the flesh, that is, fleshly temptations, but he won't have trouble with the inward man. Some teachings are really misleading; therefore, we must carefully analyze their contents. People often say that you have to die out to your old self. This is erroneous. You don't have to die out to old self when you've been born again and a new self is in place of him. That new self is the Spirit and nature of God. He is new. God doesn't think like you do unless you are born again and vice versa. The born-again child of God thinks like God. What you have to do after the new birth is to die out to the flesh. The flesh is the same body and the same flesh as it was before you were saved, but the new man who is born from God is a new man in Christ.

This new man on the inside has to be fed and the right kind of food is the Word of God. The Word of God is the only kind of food that is available in this earth to feed your spirit—the only food that will make it strong enough to believe God. Romans 10:17 says, "So then faith cometh by hearing, and hearing by the word of God."

3

Don't Ask Your Body Anything

I want to emphasize to you that your spirit won't be stronger than your body unless you read the Bible. God's Word is what feeds your spirit and gets strength into your spirit so you can have faith not to listen to your body—in other words, to the reasoning of your natural senses. Don't give in to the dictates of your body—the fleshly self—but feed the real you—the inward man—the right kind of food, which is the Word. As you do this, you will find that your faith will get stronger and stronger.

Do as Paul said. In 1 Corinthians 9:27, he stated, "But I keep under my body, and bring it into subjection: lest that by any means, when I have preached to others, I myself should be a castaway." Paul said, "I keep it under." You might say, Under what? He meant that he kept his body under the subjection of his spirit. You can't do that unless your spirit is strong, so daily feed it the Word of God.

Remember, Jesus said that you must know the truth (*see* John 8:32). *You must know it!* When you know it you can be free, and that means your body, too. You don't have to allow disease and affliction to kill your body. Your body is the house you live in—the temple of God—and why should God want His earthly temple to be diseased with an affliction from His and your enemy—the devil? God's Spirit is priceless; it is eternal. (Would you want to put a pretty, new, expensive car into an old garage that might fall in on it? Neither does God want His earthly temples to be dilapidated or diseased.)

If your house was damaged and falling down, you would have to call a contractor or a carpenter to come in and repair it and build it up strong. You wouldn't call in a medical doctor and give him some nails and a hammer and tell him to fix your house because he wouldn't know what he was doing. You wouldn't call a car dealer or a bank president in; that is not their occupation. If you want the job done efficiently, you will call in one who is qualified in the profession he follows. The same is true concerning the body in which you live. God made that body and He is the only One who is qualified to take care of it properly. He is the Creator and He knows everything about every part of it. Although many doctors are thoroughly dedicated to their profession, they still are very limited and actually know little, comparatively, about the different parts of the human body and the way they function. It often takes them months to diagnose an affliction properly and when they do it is sometimes too late, or they are not able to produce a cure, but God knows everything about it and your faith in Him can bring a cure. He spake every part of your body into existence to begin with and it is no great problem or task for Him to give a little power out to repair it, for His supply of knowledge and power cannot be exhausted.

This promise is made to you if you will only believe: Jesus said, ". . . all things are possible to him that believeth" (Mark 9:23). He also stated through His servant in Acts 10:34, "Of a truth I perceive that God is no respecter of persons." That means He has no "pets" or favorites.

Remember Paul said, "I beseech you therefore, brethren . . . that ye present your bodies. . . ." You are the boss, the custodian, the manager of your house. Why did Paul want the body presented? To make it a living sacrifice. That means total consecration and dedication; yet, this cannot be done if the body is sickly or diseased because it has little life in it to present as a living sacrifice. Paul went on to say that it should be holy and acceptable, which is your reasonable service.

God is reasonable. Present your body as a living sacrifice. Get involved with a good fundamental church which teaches the full Gospel from Matthew through Revelation. This is God's way—live holy, as Paul says. This is the only acceptable way. Present your body. Take an active part in spreading the Gospel. Put Him first in your life and all the promises of the New Testament (new covenant) are yours on this condition—the condition that you serve Him, not only with your words, but with your body. Paul says this is your reasonable service. God does not expect out of us more than we are qualified to do, but He does expect us to do that for which we are qualified.

We have often heard religious leaders say, "Well,

t doesn't make any difference about the body and what he body does, or even how it sins. The body is never going to get to heaven anyway," but I declare unto you on the authority of God's Word, it *does make all the difference in this world* to God concerning what you do with or to the body. He wants that body transformed (renewed and changed). He wants it to be a living sacrifice and to be holy, and this is the only plan or way that is acceptable to Him.

You need to understand that the Holy Spirit lives in your body after you accept Jesus as your personal Saviour, and God wants your body to be a house that the Holy Spirit can live in. Would you want to live in a filthy, dirty, germ-ridden house? Of course not! Neither does the precious Holy Spirit want to live in a sin-sick house.

Don't ask your body anything, because its desires cannot be the criterion on which it is safe to rely. It might suggest the same life and habits which you had in the past, or even new habits. Those same temptations and weak moments can come upon you and your body will want to yield to these, so you can't afford to ask your body (your fleshly self) anything. You must seek God's face and find out what He wants you to do, and not yield in any measure or any way to the carnal desires. If you do, your body will rule over the spirit— the inward man—and your spiritual man will go down in defeat.

If you allow your body to begin to break the laws of God—the Ten Commandments—thus committing sin, the Holy Spirit will leave your body because it absolutely refuses to live in an impure temple, spiritually speaking. Your faith in God's Word will not only heal you, but it can keep you strong. Claim the Scriptures which God has given you for a well body and stand on His promises securely, because heaven and earth may pass away, but His Word will never fail. Claim them now!

Your Faith Must Take Precedence Over the Senses

One morning I received a call at my home. It was from a family with whom I was acquainted. The wife was very sick. She had been to the doctor the day before and was to return that day. The woman said, "My body is full of pain and it is so messed up, I wonder if you would come and pray for me."

Since I was so rushed and had so many things on my mind that day, I forgot to go to her home. As I was driving to town to my office, suddenly the Spirit of the Lord came upon me and He said, *You didn't go pray for that woman.* So, I turned my car around at the next side road and went back to her home.

It was obvious that she was a very sick woman, for as I walked in, she appeared to be half dead with pain. She said, "I went to the doctor yesterday, but found no relief and I'm supposed to return again today."

I asked, "How much did it cost you?"

She said, "Ten dollars, plus the cost of all the medicine."

I retorted, "Well, you don't have to go back. In fact you're not going to go back because it won't be necessary."

She replied, "But Brother Norvel, you don't understand. I have such awful pain in my body and I must have help."

I answered, "Jesus is that help; He is that relief. I'm going to break that power in Jesus' name and make it leave you."

She said, "But you don't know how badly I am hurting."

I said, "Don't ask your body anything; in other words, don't look to that pain, look to Jesus."

I just took authority over that pain and disease in Jesus' name and I broke that power that was making her suffer and commanded it to go in Jesus' name as I placed my hand on her head. Immediately God's healing power began to flow through her body, and the mighty power of God began to make her shake as it surged through her being. Jesus healed her right there as she stood on the floor of her den. They were people of the Baptist faith and her husband also witnessed that Jesus healed her.

It is impossible to keep your healing so long as you yield to the symptoms of your body. Don't ask your body anything. This means don't yield to the five senses, especially the sense of pain. Rather look to God's Word and what it says and stand steadfastly with unwavering faith and command the oppressing powers that cause you to suffer to leave in Jesus' name. When they leave, God's power will begin to minister to you, and you will feel the manifestation of His healing power as it flows through you.

It was a pleasure to watch God heal her, and she didn't have to return to the doctor and pay out more money. God's healing power is so precious, so valuable, and *all things are possible to him that believeth.*

Now remember, don't ask your body how it feels or what it thinks. Rely on what God thinks and on what God says. Get your life all straightened out with His will and way and healing will be yours!

4

Jesus Talked About Your Faith

In God's Word throughout the New Testament, Jesus talked many times to people about their faith and their believing. Sometimes when a blind man would come to Jesus, Jesus would say, "Do you believe I am able to do this?" and he would say, "Yes, Lord, I believe." Then Jesus would say, "According to your faith, so be it unto you," and the blind man's eyes would immediately open (*see* Matthew 9:27-30). So often the person who is ill wants to put the responsibility on the minister or the one who is praying for him, but note in the Scriptures that Jesus shifted the responsibility of believing back to the individual. Vicarious faith is faith which one can have for another's needs or healing. Jesus never used His own faith as He is the essence of love and faith, but He always healed according to the faith of the individual for whom He was praying. The same remains true today. Vicarious faith is necessary when the person for whom we are praying is unconscious or dead, because then they cannot exercise faith. Jesus raised the dead, using His own faith; in other instances, He worked or answered according to the faith of the individual. (Concerning personal work, as for a person who is going out and passing out tracts and telling lost people about Jesus, we don't have to ask if they have faith in Jesus because they are exemplifying their faith by their actions. Faith without works is dead; therefore, it is an act of faith when we make an effort to come for healing.)

If Jesus said in the New Testament that your faith heals you, then He is still saying today that your faith heals you! The price has already been paid. Just accept it now! Your faith is an absolute requisite. *You* must do the believing and not someone else.

Notice Luke, the sixteenth chapter and seventeenth verse: Jesus said, "And it is easier for heaven and earth to pass, than one tittle of the law to fail." God's Word is irrefragable and irrevocable, that is, it cannot be refuted or disproved and it cannot be repealed or changed. It is easier for heaven and earth to pass away than for His Word to fail. There is no such thing as any part of God's Word *failing to him that believeth*.

Since "all things are possible to him that believeth" (Mark 9:23), this means it is possible for God's healing power to come into your body to straighten limbs out, open blind eyes, and heal whatever afflictions are in your body, regardless of how serious they may be. The mountain of affliction which you have in your body may be too tall to span or climb over, but you can become tall enough in God's Word to merely step over it.

I should like to pause here and say to you that if you have an affliction in your body at this time, regardless of how long you have endured it, just come to Him right now and this time come through His Word. Accept what He says because your faith in His Word can heal you.

Another important Scripture which I should like to refer you to is Mark, the fifth chapter and the twenty-eighth verse: "She said, If I may touch but his clothes, I shall be whole." The twenty-ninth verse continues, "Straightway the fountain of her blood was dried up; and she felt in her body that she was healed of that plague."

First of all, I want you to notice, she went to Him. Don't wait for Jesus to come to you because He is not coming. You have to go to Him *through His Word and through your own believing*. Verses 30 through 34 continue:

> And Jesus, immediately knowing in himself that virtue had gone out of him, turned him about in the press, and said, Who touched my clothes? And his disciples said unto him, Thou seest the multitude thronging thee, and sayest thou, Who touched me? And he looked round about to see her that had done this thing. But the woman fearing and trembling, knowing what was done in her, came and fell down before him, and told him all the truth. And he said unto her, Daughter, thy faith hath made thee whole; go in peace, and be whole of thy plague.

Now I want you to take special notice: He said, *"Thy* faith hath made thee whole." Now stop and think Think! Think! If her faith made her whole and God is no respecter of persons, then *your faith can make you whole.* If it can't, then Jesus loved this woman more than He loved you and He would have to be a respecter of persons, but He is not. He loves you just as much as He loved her. He called her "daughter" and if you are born again you are a daughter or a son, and God loves all His children the same and His love is great enough, broad enough, deep enough, and immense enough to include all His children. Yes, He loves you just as much as He did the woman in Mark, the fifth chapter. He loves you both the same. God is not the kind of God to show partiality; He loves everyone the same. Your faith puts God's love to work and He works for everybody. That includes you!

Wouldn't it grieve you or hurt you deeply if someone whom you loved doubted your word? Then you can see how God delights in you when you believe Him and take His Word. "Without faith it is impossible to please God" (*see* Hebrews 11:6). That means it is impossible to find favor in His sight. It is an insult to Him for you to doubt His Word. Satan is a liar and the "father of lies" (*see* John 8:44), but God's Word is Truth!

Are you ashamed to tell people that Jesus is the Healer? Are you ashamed to study the Scriptures in the Bible that tell what God said concerning faith? If you are ashamed, and ashamed to come to Him, then you are not going to be healed. Much that people have been taught is junk because it is only an erroneous conception of man's ideas, but the Truth must triumph over all.

Jesus declared, "I am the way, the truth, and the

life. . . ." (John 14:6). Jesus is the Truth and there is no other truth anywhere else, except it be based on His Word. So, whatever part of God's Word you deny or which you are ashamed of, this is the part that you can't have.

It is a sad, terrible, and disgusting thing to have sickness in your body and to be lying flat on your back, just withering away day after day and year after year when God, through His Son Jesus, has made it possible for you to be healed. What a waste of power—God's power! God is God! God doesn't change! God doesn't fail! God doesn't lie or make false promises which He cannot keep! It simply does not matter what people think, not even those closest to you. It is what God's Word says that actually counts! God is counting on you. Why don't you count on His Word? The only part of God's Word that will ever help you is the Word that you know for yourself. This not only means saving words, but this also means healing words. Your faith, being strong enough to believe His Word without wavering, brings healing to your body.

God wants you to deny your own ways and accept His. Luke 9:23 states: "If any man will come after me, let him deny himself. . . ." (That means to deny the things which your body wants if they are contrary to God's will and ways.)

. . . and take up his cross daily, and follow me. For whosoever will save his life shall lose it: but whosoever will lose his life for my sake, the same shall save it. For what is a man advantaged, if he gain the whole

world, and lose himself, or be a cast away? For whosoever shall be ashamed of me and of my words [this
includes healing words], of him shall the Son of man
be ashamed, when he shall come in his own glory, and
in his Father's, and of the holy angels.

Luke 9:23-26

"For whosoever shall be ashamed of me and of my
words. . . ." This also means healing words. So, don't
be ashamed of God's Word, regardless of what it
teaches. If you are, God will be ashamed of you and
will deny you as His child on the great day of reckon-
ing.

The twenty-seventh verse of that chapter states, "But
I tell you of a truth, there be some standing here, which
shall not taste of death, till they see the kingdom of
God." When we do God's will, we become subjects of
His kingdom, thus a part of His kingdom and an heir
of His kingdom. That means an heir to all that God
owns and that includes His healing power for our bodies,
but we must be willing to deny ourselves to the point
that we put His kingdom and the advancement of that
kingdom first in our lives. ". . . and take up his cross
daily. . . ." Jesus bore the cross, not for Himself, nor
for His sins, but for others. Likewise, if we would become an intrinsic part of that kingdom, we must be
willing to share the burdens and needs of others.

God wants you to "die" now so that you can "live"
now. He who loses his life shall save it. Die out to self
and refuse to feed your body things of the world. If

you don't, the devil will attack you, and you will become vulnerable to his tactics.

If you give your body to the devil he will have the right-of-way to attack. God does not want to give your energy to some religious organization which does not teach the Truth; neither does He want you to give of your time and means.

In the next chapter I will relate to you the true story of what happened to members of my family because they had never been taught the divine truths of God concerning healing and how to act on God's promises.

5

My Mother Died at Age Thirty-seven

I should like to point out to you that some people will try to teach you that people don't die until God is ready for them to die. I should like to say to you that this theory is not in line with the teaching of God's Word. This concept or theory is a lie from the devil. I realize that many who believe this are honest-hearted Christians, but you can still be a Christian and believe what the devil tells you about your body. He will tell you all kinds of things, but only God's Word is the Truth.

My mother was a Christian woman. She loved Jesus with all her heart. She went to church all the time when I was a little child. When my mother reached the age of thirty-seven, I was ten years of age. By then she had already spent lots of time in doctors' offices and in hospitals, and had undergone operations. She had numerous tumors in her body and she died at the age of thirty-seven.

As a little, cotton-headed boy at the age of ten, I thought that either God killed her or that it was God's will for her to die. Because my mother loved and served Jesus, I didn't know or consider the fact that the devil had anything to do with her death.

About four years later, there was another tragic death in our family, and I didn't understand this because the church we were attending put the sick people's names on the blackboard every Sunday morning and remembered to pray for them.

While my mother was ill the people prayed, "Heal Mrs. Hayes, Lord, if it be Thy will," but what they were actually saying was, "Lord, if it is not Thy will to heal her, then just go ahead and let her die, or just go ahead and kill her." I couldn't understand this kind of praying because I was too small.

After I grew up and received Jesus into my heart and started to study the Bible, I found out that this kind of praying for the sick people was caused by doubt and unbelief and that it was not scriptural.

Jesus will heal people only one way and that is through faith, and He will heal anyone who trusts Him. *Jesus doesn't allow His healing power to come into your body until He is pleased with your faith.*

Now the Bible teaches us how to pray for the sick people; therefore, let us explore its contents: In the Book of James, chapter 5, verses 14 and 15, it states:

Is any sick among you? let him call for the elders of the church; and let them pray over him, anointing him with oil in the name of the Lord: And the prayer of faith shall save the sick, and the Lord shall raise him up; and if he have committed sins, they shall be forgiven him.

It is just as easy for Jesus to heal as it is for Him to save. The prayer of faith is all that is necessary.

Jesus said in Mark 11:24, "What things soever ye desire, when ye pray, believe that ye receive them, and ye shall have them." Not maybe, sometimes, but every time, and NOW! Not later, but *when you pray.*

In Mark 16:17 and 18, Jesus gave out His Great Commission (or command) to the believers concerning the work that He was leaving the church (every born-again believer) to do. He commanded,". . . lay hands on the sick, and they shall recover." This command concerning the sick and their needs was not just given to the ministers alone, but to every believer, and His promise is, "They shall recover."

The church I attended, the one in which I grew up and the one which my mother attended, did not obey these Scriptures. The people prayed with their lips only, not really exercising any faith, and they said, "Lord, heal Mrs. Hayes if it be Thy will."

Mrs. Hayes died. As a ten-year-old boy, I just thought, "Well, it must not be God's will to heal her." I didn't know about the Scriptures in the Book of James, 5:14 and 15 where James says, "Is any sick among you?. . ." or that this Scripture also included my mother. But she had never been taught to call the elders of the church and tell them to bring a bottle of oil and anoint and pray the prayer of faith around her bed, and she had never been taught to say with her mouth, "Because God promised me, He will raise me up" (up is opposite of down). She had never been taught to put her faith in those two verses and trust

God, so she died prematurely. Anyone who would say that it was God's will for her to be sick and to die and leave her family, who needed her so badly, would make God to be a cruel God, but God is not that kind of a God. He is a God of love and He loves to heal people, but He can't unless they first believe, and they can't believe unless they read and stand on God's promises.

God demands that His requirements be met and Jesus demands that the last chapter of the Book of Mark be obeyed. He said ". . . lay hands on the sick, and they shall recover." That is God's way. Man's way is to pray a little prayer and lay hands off. That is the reason that we are in trouble—that so many die before their time. God not only promised health, but He promised, in the Old Testament, long life to those who obey His laws and believe His words.

If you have much knowledge of the Bible at all, you know that the New Testament is an even better covenant than the old one is under which to live. We are now living under the New Testament or covenant. It has even greater promises in it. It has easier ways and details, easier instructions to show how we can receive power from the spirit world, where God is the Boss, so we can avail ourselves of that power to help ourselves and our fellow man. I didn't know this at the time. I discovered these truths later, but it wasn't until after another tragedy struck our home.

My brother died at the age of nineteen. He was a football player in high school and I thought the same thing about him. I thought it must have been God's will for him to die, too, because people prayed the same way. They said, "Heal Glen Hayes if it be Thy will," but we buried him. I didn't know that these Scriptures were life for the human body.

After I turned my life over to God in prayer, I sought Him once for three days concerning these two deaths— my brother's death and my mother's death.

The next chapter will explain what I received on the third day of prayer from the throne of God, but first let me remind you again: God didn't put these Scriptures in this chapter for just a few. God is trying to explain to you through the Bible, as is stated in His Word: "My people perish for the lack of knowledge" (*see* Proverbs 29:18). This means for the lack of knowledge of what God's Word actually and literally says. God wants you to be informed and live an abundant life!

6

God Talked With Me About My Mother's Death

As I stated in the previous chapter, my mother died at the age of thirty-seven, when I was ten years of age. After I grew up and got into the business world, I became quite successful in my businesses. Soon they began to enlarge and I also acquired other businesses. As a businessman I like to see credits instead of debits on my profit-and-loss statements at the end of the month.

The same applies to the spiritual realm. I couldn't find anywhere in the New Testament where God put diseases in His children's bodies. If I hired an employee and he was a good employee, I promoted him. God does the same thing with His children. If we stay in line with the Word, we enjoy the benefits thereof.

My mother was a good Christian woman. She loved Jesus and loved the church and loved people. She loved to pray and work for Jesus, but I didn't realize then that unscriptural praying could bring death into your body. I didn't realize that unscriptural praying left the door open for the devil to attack your body even though your spirit was in tune with Jesus; I didn't realize that the Holy Spirit who lives in your body only works in line with the confession of the Scriptures and that the confession has to be in faith.

I knew that my mother was a good worker for Jesus and would win souls and it didn't make any sense to me that God would kill her at the age of thirty-seven, when she was winning souls for the kingdom of God all the time. She was constantly telling people about Jesus. She would pray for them until they became convicted of their sins and would give their lives over to God. I didn't know that the devil did this to my mother and to my brother. I went to God in prayer and started praying to the Lord and saying unto Him, "Now Jesus, I don't want to pray wrong. If I am praying out of line, I want You to forgive me for it. Since I am a businessman, liking credits instead of debits, it really doesn't make sense to me why You killed my mother. You said that one soul is worth more than the whole world and my mother was winning souls for the kingdom and You killed her at the age of thirty-seven. If You had let her live to the age of sixty-five or seventy-five, she would have won a lot more souls and it really just doesn't make sense to me, so I would like to ask You why You did it because I don't understand it. But Jesus, I don't want You to get angry with me. After all, it was my mother and I needed her and if You will be kind enough to tell me, I would like to know why You did it."

On the third day of prayer the Word of the Lord came unto me saying, *Son, I didn't kill your mother; I didn't have anything to do with it,* and that statement was surely a shock to me.

Jesus said further unto me: *I tell you in My Word that death is My enemy. I do not go around putting diseases and sicknesses in people's bodies. The devil does that. I didn't put those tumors in your mother's body. The devil attacked her body. The tumors in your mother's body were what killed her, but they didn't come from heaven because there are not any here. No sicknesses or diseases are given out to the human race by God, the Father, or by Me because there is no sickness here to be given out. I tell you in My Word that all good things come down from heaven and your mother couldn't receive divine healing for her body because she didn't know how.*

The reason that she didn't know how was that she had never been taught how to receive God's healing power for her body. She had never been taught to obey the contents of the healing verses in the New Testament. The promises in there don't work automatically. They come to you through your faith in God's Word because God *is* the Word, God *was* the Word, and God *will always be* the Word. God and the Word are the same.

Remember, son, He said to me, *people can't believe something that they haven't been taught.*

I said, "Yes, Lord, that is right; people can't believe something which they haven't been taught."

All of the teachings of the New Testament and the provisions that have been made in heaven for the human race are for anybody. No church and no individual can enjoy the provisions God has made for the human race unless they believe, and they cannot believe unless their faith in the Scriptures is strong enough.

It is not good enough to try to build your faith on what you have heard or what somebody told you. If you belong to a church or have friends who don't obey the Scriptures, such as the last chapter of the Book of Mark where Jesus said, ". . . lay hands on the sick, and they shall recover," and James 5:14, ". . . anointing him with oil in the name of the Lord," so that God's healing power will be imparted to you, then you should find a church which teaches the full Gospel (Good News) of God's power.

If you say out loud, "Mountain, be moved from my body; tumors, be removed from my body; cancer, be removed from my body," and will doubt not, and tell the mountain to be removed from your life, from your body, and if you believe, those things which you say shall come to pass, for Jesus said, ". . . he shall have whatsoever he saith" (Mark 11:23).

I never did see these Scriptures practiced when I was growing up. I saw people get saved and join the church, but I never did see any faith being put into the verses which called for the healing of the body. Of course the Lord let me know in no uncertain terms that no human being could jump over the Word and believe what they wanted to believe and receive God's benefits.

God is the Truth and there is no other truth. God wants you to open up your ears and let your heart be receptive unto His promises. If you will put your trust in what God says, your faith can heal you. The Bible says, "Faith cometh by hearing, and hearing by the word of God" (Romans 10:17). You might say, "What is faith?" God's Word says in Hebrews 11:1, "Now faith is. . . ." If it is not now, then it is not faith and it doesn't work! "Now faith is the substance of things hoped for, the evidence of things not seen." You can't wait until you have seen a disease healed before you believe God's Word.

You have allowed your life to be bound up in too much natural bondage in your own way of living. It is hard for you to understand the ways of God. You should have been feeding your faith in the former verses upon God's Word, but if you haven't, it is not too late to return wholeheartedly to His Word and fling yourself upon it for deliverance.

Your faith in God's Word will heal you only if you act upon it. If you haven't really trusted in God's Word in the past, just repent and tell Jesus that you are sorry and start studying the Scriptures recorded in this book and then begin to claim them for your body and begin to say with your mouth, "I accept God's healing power for my body and I believe that I will receive what I pray for. I realize, Jesus, that You love me as much as You loved the woman who was dying in the fifth chapter of the Book of Mark."

You will either get your thinking straightened out by God's Word or you are not going to receive. You are not going to make God do anything, but your faith can heal you. Your faith in the Scriptures can heal you. Yes, it is God's will for your body to be healthy.

Absolute Protection for Those Who Trust in God

God not only promised health for your body and His power for your healing, protection from disease, and victory over the enemy in the Old Testament, but

He also promised constant, divine protection. In the Ninety-First Psalm it says:

He that dwelleth in the secret place of the most High shall abide under the shadow of the Almighty. I will say of the Lord, He is my refuge and my fortress: my God; in him will I trust. Surely he shall deliver thee from the snare of the fowler, and from the noisome pestilence. He shall cover thee with his feathers, and under his wings shalt thou trust: his truth shall be thy shield and buckler. Thou shalt not be afraid for the terror by night; nor for the arrow that flieth by day; Nor for the pestilence that walketh in darkness; nor for the destruction that wasteth at noonday. A thousand shall fall at thy side, and ten thousand at thy right hand; but it shall not come nigh thee. Only with thine eyes shalt thou behold and see the reward of the wicked. Because thou hast made the Lord, which is my refuge, even the most High, thy habitation; There shall no evil befall thee, neither shall any plague come nigh thy dwelling. For he shall give his angels charge over thee, to keep thee in all thy ways. They shall bear thee up in their hands, lest thou dash thy foot against a stone. Thou shalt tread upon the lion and adder: the young lion and the dragon shalt thou trample under feet. Because he hath set his love upon me, therefore will I deliver him: I will set him on high, because he hath known my name. He shall call upon me, and I will answer him: I will be with him in trouble; I will deliver him, and honour him. With long life will I satisfy him, and shew him my salvation.

In these Scriptures God has promised the following to those who wholeheartedly and unreservedly trust Him. He promised: refuge and protection; prosperity (protection from pestilence which destroys the crops); freedom from fear; protection from the robber and thief; protection from demon forces ("them that walk in darkness" [*see* Psalms 91:6]); protection in battle ("A thousand shall fall at thy side . . ." [verse 7]); victory over your enemies, and even the attention and divine care of His holy angels (*see* verse 11).

Notice in the fifteenth and sixteenth verses of this Ninety-First Psalm, He even promises deliverance from trouble, the right to call on His name at any time, honor, and long life. What more could anyone need?

Fear and trouble put people in the hospital and even drive people insane, but this is not God's will for the human race. There are many people who live in constant fear which is so great that their lives become a burden. Jesus came to break this bondage. Claim all the promises just listed in the Ninety-First Psalm. Claim them out loud. Believe first and the manifestation (proof of His power) will come later.

God's promises are all conditional. If we "abide under the shadow of the Almighty" (Psalms 91:1), we are living close to Him.

And Jesus came and spake unto them, saying, All power is given unto me in heaven and in earth. Go ye therefore, and teach all nations . . . whatsoever I have commanded you: and, lo, I am with you alway, even unto the end of the world.

Matthew 28:18-20

Don't worry about Jesus leaving you; Don't worry about God's healing power working for you. Jesus plainly said that He had all power in heaven and earth, so His power is available on earth and *it is available to you!*

Jesus Christ is the indisputable Victor; He met Satan on his grounds and wrestled the keys of death, hell, and the grave from him, then He cried out, ". . . because I live, ye shall live also" (John 14:19), and, "Behold, I give unto you power to tread on serpents and scorpions, and over all the power of the enemy: and nothing shall by any means hurt you" (Luke 10:19).

"All the power of the enemy" includes power over sickness, power over diseases, and power over sin and the enemy of our soul—the devil. This authority is relegated to every believer, without reservation. God's power is inexhaustive!

The same God who spake the world into existence, the same God who spake the parts of your body into existence, the same God who gave His authority to His believers will also speak and bring health back to your body. Believe now! Accept it by faith; confess it with your mouth out loud!

Again, notice the Book of Matthew, chapter 21, verse 22: Jesus said, "And all things, whatsoever ye shall ask in prayer, believing, ye shall receive." He said "all things." I repeat, *all things!* Believe *now* as you ask for it. Don't waver in your faith. (To waver means to be tossed back and forth; to vacillate between two opinions or two forces.) Don't be tossed and torn by the two forces of belief and unbelief. Don't waver! Don't fear! Don't doubt! Believe!

James 1:6 states, "But let him ask in faith, nothing wavering. For he that wavereth is like a wave of the sea driven with the wind and tossed." God's Word is your compass. Be stabilized or established in His Word.

You can walk out of that bed by God's power. God loves you and He wants you to receive that power and He wants you to accept it now! Psalms 50:23 states, ". . . to him that ordereth his conversation aright will I show the salvation of God." Start talking faith; start talking health; start talking what the Bible says; start talking what you believe. You are healed because the Word says you are!

The price for healing has already been paid, just as the price for your salvation has been paid, but it is yours to accept or reject. The price was paid by Jesus as He bore the stripes in your place (*see* Isaiah 53:5). Don't let the devil steal it away from you through erroneous ideas. It doesn't make any difference what the devil says or what your relatives think. If you base your belief on their opinions or sentiments there is little hope for you now or ever to recover. As Jesus bore those cruel lashes in Pilate's hall, you were healed. "He was wounded for our transgressions, he was bruised for our iniquities: the chastisement of our peace was upon him; and with his stripes we are healed" (Isaiah 53:5). This was prophesied of Jesus Christ and when He came to earth He fulfilled that prophesy in Pilate's hall. He drank the bitter cup of suffering down to the last dreg of pain and even to death, that we might be free from sin, that we might have peace, and that we might be healed. Notice that healing was the first provision He made for our redemption. He was beaten and by those stripes you were healed. He was beaten before He was crucified. He died for our sins, but He was beaten for our sicknesses. "You were healed" includes you, and you, and you! Believe it! Say it! Act upon it! Do this now and the victory will be yours!

7

Baptist Boy Healed by Believing Mark

I have a good personal friend who was raised as a Baptist, just as I was, but when he was born, he was born prematurely. The parts of his body were deformed because they never developed. His blood was never right because he weighed less than two pounds when he was born. The doctor said that he would stay that way for a few short years, and when he became a teen-ager he would die.

The only thing he ever heard preached was salvation. Sometimes he also attended the Christian church, but that church didn't preach divine healing through the power of God, either.

He grew up in a Southern Baptist home, was taught the way of salvation through faith in the Lord Jesus Christ, but he didn't understand about divine healing. As a result of this lack of knowledge concerning the healing of his body, this deformed friend had suffered all his life, and when he became a teen-ager he was lying on his deathbed without a ray of hope for his body.

Five doctors, one of whom had practiced with the great Mayo Clinic, pronounced his case as absolutely hopeless. As far as medical science was concerned, to the doctors' knowledge, no one in his condition had ever lived past sixteen years of age.

Soon he became bedfast and began to just wither away. It seemed that death was very near. In this condition, with all the hope in the ability of man's skill completely gone, he began to turn to God's Word for comfort. He asked for a Bible and he began reading from the first Gospel in the New Testament—the Book of Matthew. Since he was paralyzed and almost blind, he could only read for a short while each day. It was almost impossible for him to carry on a conversation, as he would stammer and stutter so. His case was pathetic indeed!

After several days, he finally read through the Book of Matthew, then he began to read from the second Gospel—the Book of Mark. He was keenly attracted by a special verse which he found in the eleventh chapter. It was the twenty-fourth verse where Jesus stated, "Therefore I say unto you [little deformed, crippled boy, or anyone else], What things soever ye desire, when ye pray, believe that ye receive them, and ye shall have them."

As he read this verse, hope began to rise in his heart, so he read it over and over again. Finally he said, "Jesus, since You haven't told a lie here in this verse, I am coming out of this bed. You said, 'Whatsoever you desire,' and I desire to come off this bed." He continued, "Lord, You know I desire to go to heaven, but I also desire to have a well, strong body like other boys, and You said I could have what I desire. I am going to pray and I am going to believe and I am going to receive."

Eleven months went by and nothing happened. He

waited night after night for God to come and heal him, but it never happened because he didn't understand how to release his faith.

In desperation he asked for several ministers to come to his house, as he wanted to ask them if Jesus really meant what He said in Mark 11:24. Three ministers were sent for, two of whom never came. Finally, after several days, the third minister came.

The minister went into his room where he was lying on the bed, and obviously the minister was shocked at the sight he saw, for the lad was almost a skeleton—just skin and bones, over six feet tall and only weighing eighty-nine pounds. It seemed that he would soon take his last breath. He had been lying there for sixteen months, just holding on day after day, grasping for the least straw of hope.

With his stammering and stuttering, he laboriously tried to ask the minister if Jesus meant what He said in Mark 11:24. The minister, thinking the boy couldn't talk, picked up his hand, patted it, and said in a sober, professionally pious voice, "Just be patient, my boy. In a few days it will all be over." Then the minister laid down his hand, turned around slowly, and walked out of the room.

My Baptist friend said that he put out all the light of the little ray of hope that he had. He only added to the boy's discouragement, leaving him more despondent and confused than ever. It was very dark in that room— all the light he had hoped for had been put out. He still weeps today when he tells it.

The minister walked back out to the living room and began to have prayer for the family, asking God to be

kind to them and to give them comfort in that time
of bereavement and seemingly inevitable death of their
loved one. My friend could hear the minister praying
from the front of the house, and suddenly, as he heard
this prayer, it seemed his spirit wanted to scream out,
"I am not dead yet! Do you understand me? I'm not
dead yet! I am not dead!"

After the minister left, the relatives came in and
asked him, "Son, what kind of flowers do you want
for your funeral?"

He stuttered out, "It doesn't make any difference.
I won't be able to see them."

Then they asked, "Whom do you want for your
minister and for pallbearers and what songs do you want
sung?"

He replied, "It doesn't make any difference; I won't
be able to hear them anyway."

According to the conversation of the minister and
relatives, they almost had him buried and he was still
breathing. They promised him a good funeral.

The way of man is not the way of God. The ways
of man will put out the light of your hope many times,
especially if you are deformed or afflicted with a hope-
lessly incurable disease. You must not look through
the natural eyes of man if you are in this condition, but
rather look through the eyes of God and behold the
light of His Word.

Do you realize that the best and most qualified doctors in the land can look at you and say, "There is no
hope," and the most qualified minister in the land,
from an educational standpoint, can look at you and

say, "There is no hope"; yet, right in the middle of all that, God's Spirit can shine through that dismal cloud of hopelessness and penetrate it with God's Word, which states, "By His stripes you are healed." All the darkness in the world cannot put out the light of one little candle; neither can all the doubt in the world prevent your healing if you yourself don't put out your ray of hope in God's eternal Word by unbelief.

The Bible teaches that faith without works (action) is dead (*see* James 2:17). You must understand this and keep it in your memory forever. This young, deformed friend had to learn the lesson of active faith before he could be healed. The Word of God is carried to our hearts and spirit by the power of the Holy Ghost. The Holy Ghost—the Third Person of the Godhead—is here to help you, and the Holy Ghost, who is not only a Comforter but also a great Teacher, was present to lead my friend into the truths of God's Holy Word.

This Baptist friend then began to read from the fifth chapter of Mark, where the Holy Spirit opened up another divine secret to him. He read that the woman with the incurable issue of blood said, "If I may touch but his clothes, I shall be [made] whole" (verse 28). He read that she forced her way into the crowd with her weakened body, but with an unwavering faith to receive that which she so desperately had to have. He read that by her own effort she touched His clothes and released her faith and that immediately Jesus rewarded that faith by allowing His healing virtue to flow into her body. (It only took one touch from Jesus!) As he read this, his faith began to rise again and he discovered that he must put forth a natural effort, that he must act upon God's Word, because then he realized that faith without works is dead. Slowly he began to realize that if he wanted a miracle in his life he must use his own faith, and not someone else's faith, and he must put forth some action himself.

I want to tell you, my friend, that faith must have action mixed with it. Faith without action is dead! You have to believe it is true, you have to say it is true, and you also must act like it is true. God doesn't tell lies. His Word is not fictitious. He doesn't make up stories for entertainment. He means business! If you really mean business and really want healing, and not merely sympathy, then follow these three simple steps: Believe! Say! Act!

As this deformed lad began to comprehend the truth of active faith, he took his elbows and pushed one paralyzed leg off the side of the bed and it hit the floor like a chunk of wood. He then reached over with his elbows and wiggled around and pushed the other leg off. He had no feeling in either leg, so it also fell as if it were a chunk of wood. With great and strained effort he worked around and finally mustered enough strength to push his body off the bed and onto the floor. It fell with a thud, but nothing happened. He began to make his way to the foot of the bed with his elbows, dragging his dead body along. As he locked his arms around the foot of the bed, he said, "Jesus, You said in Mark 11:23 that we can have what we say. If I don't doubt You in my heart, anything I say will come to pass—I can have whatever I say. And You said in the next verse, Mark 11:24, 'What things soever ye desire, when ye pray, believe that ye receive them, and ye shall have them.' I believe in my heart that You've heard my prayer. I believe in my heart that I have received healing for my body—and I'm saying it with my mouth." He then began to scream with his mouth in his own voice, "Mark 11:24 is mine! I believe I have my healing! I believe I am healed! I believe I am healed because Mark 11:24 says I am healed. Mark 11:24 is mine! I've got it! Mark 11:24 is mine! I've got it! I've got it! I confess with my mouth that it is mine! I confess it before God, and in the face of the devil and in front of anybody else who asks me that the contents of Mark 11:24 are mine! Thank God for a well body! Thank You, Jesus, for a well body! Mark 11:24 is mine!"

While he was screaming this he said it was as if someone was standing over him pouring out a jar of warm honey, because it tasted sweet going down through his body. Then it seemed to be slowly running down his face and over his eyes and when it ran over his eyes, he could see well. It went down through his neck and into his shoulders, down through his body, and it came to his heart and a new heart popped into his chest. The organs that were deformed straightened out and became perfect organs in his body. Then it went down into his waist and feeling came into his body down through his paralyzed legs and his legs became strong and straight and feeling and life came back to them. It went out his feet and he had feeling and perfect blood all throughout his body and all the parts of his body were restored to normal.

He stood straight up in the middle of the floor and walked off. He has been walking ever since. He has been telling people that Jesus healed him, and he has not been ashamed to give his testimony to anyone, anywhere. (It is very important that we confess our salvation and our healing before man because the Bible, in the Book of Revelation, teaches us that we overcome by the word of our testimony and the blood of the Lamb [_see_ Revelation 12:11].) For this reason, and to encourage others to believe, he has been telling people the good news of God's healing power everywhere.

But you must remember that the contents of Mark 11:24 are not just for him. If he had not stood on those promises tenaciously and unmovably, he would have died long ago; likewise many hopeless cases will soon die unless they learn these great scriptural truths and believe and act upon them just as he did. He was not willing to take no for an answer, and we do not have to take no for an answer when God says yes. But remember, you must say yes also. "Yes" faith connects you with omnipotence. It channels you into the miracle world of heaven's power.

Jesus said, "What things soever you desire, when you pray, believe that you receive them, and you shall have them" (see Mark 11:24). Jesus spelled that Y-O-U! That means you who are reading this book! Believe right now and you shall be set free from the bondage of Satan.

Jesus said, ". . . all things are possible to him that believeth" (Mark 9:23); "Ask, and it shall be given you . . ." (Matthew 7:7); and He also said, ". . . ye have not, because ye ask not" (James 4:2). So ask Him right now and begin to thank Him out loud for your healing, for the answer to your prayers, regardless of what it is, because whatever the need may be, God will answer if you are asking in His will and it is His will for you to be healed. Thank God out loud for the answer right now! Praise Him! The doctor may have told you that your disease is incurable and that you will soon have to die, but you don't have to die.

I want to give you a word of warning right here: Don't let Satan come and steal the Word away from you. That is one of his favorite tricks—to get you so enamored with other things and the cares of life that he will take the Word of God from your mind and lips. He will even try to put the pain and symptoms back in your body to get you to doubt your healing. He is a poor loser, but he will continue to lose if you keep looking to God's Word and quoting His promises out loud and continue to thank God for your healing.

At the time of the writing of this book, I am in Wichita, Kansas, at the Holiday Inn Plaza, on the thirteenth floor. I have myself locked in this room. I have been here for hours and hours before the Lord writing this book. I told a friend at the airport when he picked me up that God wanted me to do something.

I spoke at the banquet last night here in the auditoruim. Four people came forth to be saved; one was a businessman, one was a mother, and the other two were Catholic sisters. They didn't know for sure that the Holy Spirit lived inside them, but they knew for sure before they left, as God's sweet presence ministered unto them. Between fifty and sixty came forth for healing for their bodies and God's healing presence and power was there to heal. In fact, His power became so strong that many were slain under the power of God and they lay on the floor as God's power operated on their bodies. After a while, the healing power of God became so strong in me that I felt as if my legs had turned to rubber. The power was surging through my being so strongly that my body became weak and two men had to stand on either side of me to hold me up so I could finish praying for the people.

God's healing power is strong and mighty and it is available for the human body, to heal it and to use it to pray for others, but such anointing as I had last night will sap the energy and natural strength from your body.

Some time ago I was sitting close to a crippled woman and she just got up and walked off, healed by God's mighty power. As she walked away pushing her wheelchair, in which she had been wheeled in, and as she pushed it back to the ambulance, I broke down and began to cry. I was not weeping because I was sad, but because I had been so touched by the love and power of God and what He had done for her in performing that great miracle. Oh, God's power is so sweet, so real, so strong, so wonderful! Don't let Satan steal that beautiful power from your body. It is the manifestation of God's divine presence in your life. It crushes and defeats the power of Satan—the power of sin, the power of his disease, the power of his fear, and you no longer have to be a slave to sorrow and sickness. No wonder Satan tries to get you to disbelieve it! He hates you because you are God's child. He can't strike back at God, or even touch God, because Jesus destroyed his works potentially and became the uncontested Victor, but he will continue striking back at God's children. God's Word, power, and blood will be your shield. Use these against his attacks.

God is now pouring out His Spirit upon the earth and revealing His Word to His people as I personally have never seen it before. As we are obeying Jesus' command, which Mark gave us in chapter sixteen, the devils are screaming out at us in anger because we take authority in the name of Jesus Christ and command them to leave the body of those whom they're been tormenting.

Often I would come to a sick person who had been sick for a long time and whose body, and sometimes mind also, had been disturbed by the devil. As I would take authority over that power of darkness, which is trying to destroy the human race, and as I would break it in the name of Jesus Christ, this would make the demons mad and they would come out, screaming in anger because they had to leave through the power of that name. Demons are disembodied evil spirits who seek a human body to dwell in and to torment. Because they are such hateful spirits, they can only find happiness and satisfaction in tormenting the human race—God's creation, which they so violently hate and wish to destroy and take to their last and final abode— the lake of fire (*see* Revelation 21:8). They are powerful beings, but we as believers have the authority over them in the name of Jesus, and many of us are taking that authority. We as believers need not fear them, but we must fear sin.

God is unfolding and revealing His Word to us today in such a beautiful way for the salvation of the lost, the sick, and the weak, but I want to warn you right here again: we must live holy lives and we must not let Satan steal the Word of God from our hearts or we will be helpless before the mighty onslaughts of the demon world and its consequent sin, sickness, and disease.

Not only will Mark 11:24 work for you, but the Scriptures all through the New Testament will work for you. Satan tries to prevent people from reading their Bibles, and from attending churches where the full Gospel is preached, and when people do finally hear the truth, he then comes to try to steal away what Word they have heard. Jesus said that the sower sows the Word and Satan comes immediately to take away the Word which was sown (*see* Matthew 13). Satan has no defense against the Word of God. He has no defense against the Lordship of Jesus or the name of Jesus. He has no defense against the born-again believer if that believer is walking in fact, living right, and acting on the Word of God.

Jesus said, "All power is given unto me in heaven and in earth" (Matthew 28:18). Satan has been stripped of his powers. Jesus turned those powers over to the Church, and when you are born again of the Spirit of God, you become a part of that great Church. It isn't confined to any one denomination, but is given to every truly born-again person who will accept that power and use it to God's glory.

Jesus said to His followers, "I will give unto thee the

keys of the kingdom . . ." (Matthew 16:19). But these "keys" of faith and His Word, and faith in that Word, will do us no good unless we use them. As a part of His great church, let us use the keys of the kingdom. If we build the church that Jesus wants to be built, it will be a church which is built upon His Word—all His Word. It won't be a church which believes only part of the Bible and denies the rest of it.

When Jesus went away He gave command and left His authority to the Church. I am not speaking of the church that doesn't believe in divine healing, or casting out devils, or the Baptism in the Holy Spirit, or being saved (born again by God's Spirit); I am speaking of the true Church that believes the whole Bible, whatever it says. God's power is only available to that kind of church. God's power is only available to the Bible-believing churches. Those who don't believe in these divine trusts of God's Word are merely "playing house" with their endless rituals, ceremonies, and formalities. Satan doesn't fear that kind of church; he only laughs at it, but he is afraid of the true Church, where divine authority in God is taken over his kingdom of darkness, where diseases are cast out, where demons are cast out, and where people get saved and quit the sinning business once and for all.

God's business is the most important business on earth. He left His disciples (His followers) in charge of it. His business is to break the power of Satan over people's minds, bodies, and spirits, that they might become fit subjects of the kingdom of God. If it is the most important business on earth, then why do so many

so-called ministers of the Gospel either neglect or
ignore it? Why do they give first place to doctrines of
men, programs, committee meetings, etc.? Why have
they allowed Satan to sidetrack them from the real
purpose of the ministry and from the responsibilities
of the believers to carry out the Great Commission of
Mark 16? We must have an old-fashioned returning
to all the Word of God!

You see, the devil would like to get people to stay
satisfied and complacent and set in their own ways. He
operates this way many times through the church.
Things that often seem appropriate and look good and
which are appealing to the populace are often only de-
vices, which are comparable to a "wolf in a sheep's
clothing." It is a deception of Satan. Denominations
which adhere to such have no real power of God to
deliver a lost world from the clutches of Satan. They
become mere moral social orders, and sometimes not
even so moral, which means they are only social orders,
nothing more than some philanthropic club. This is a
sick church and it needs healing itself before it can help
bring deliverance to a lost and dying world. A person
cannot deliver another from bondage if he is in bondage himself. He must first break his bonds through his
faith and belief in God's Word, or he can never be
qualified to break the bonds of others. A blind man
is not qualified to lead another blind man, lest they
both fall in a ditch together. Only God's Word can
cure that blindness!

Some churches and people only believe part of God's
Word. *The part you don't believe is the part that you*

can never have! Why not believe it all? Why not believe and enjoy the full benefits of Calvary, which was purchased by His own stripes and by the shedding of His own blood? Why cheat yourself?

The basic principle of the Christian life is to know that God put sin, sickness, disease, sorrow, grief, and poverty on Jesus at Calvary. For Him to put any of this on us now would be a miscarriage of justice. Jesus, who was sinless, was made a curse (willing to become sin) that we might receive the beautiful blessings of Abraham, the father of the faithful. Glory be to God forevermore! Jesus died for the whole human race. He willed His righteousness and authority to us. All we have to do is just take it! Take it by faith in His name.

We have read in James, chapter 1, verse 8, that a double-minded person is unstable in all his ways. A double-minded person is like a person who is trying to ride two horses at the same time. He will eventually be torn asunder. This is the mental state of those who are double-minded. They are trying to serve two masters at the same time, and consequently they will also be torn asunder. If a man is double-minded he will fall. If he imagines, assumes, or in any way has the idea that God is behind his troubles, he will never resist Satan.

In Mark 3:24 and 25, Jesus stated, "And if a kingdom be divided against itself, that kingdom cannot stand. And if a house be divided against itself, that house cannot stand." If God delights in afflictions of His people and if He brings these on His followers, who make up His kingdom, spiritually, then God is divided against Himself and His kingdom cannot stand, but God's Word informs us that His kingdom will stand forever.

Sickness, fear, and sin are tools of the devil. God does not condescend to use the tools of Satan; His kingdom is a kingdom of love, joy, and peace in the Holy Ghost. Satan's kingdom brings torments. He is a warped personality who is twisted and crazy in his thinking and he wants his subjects—his followers—to be as he is.

Satan has absolutely no authority whatever against God's eternal Word and he knows that, but so long as he can fool you and talk you out of believing God's Word and acting upon it, he will keep you from the victory.

God does not use Satan to discipline His family. (If your child disobeyed you to the point that corrective discipline was necessary, would you do it yourself in love as it should be done or would you allow some evil reprobate or criminal to come and chastise your child and beat him or her in line? The answer is obvious.)

What is the chastisement of the Lord? Does God use Satan to punish His family? Study the Old and New Testaments concerning this subject and you will find that God never put sicknesses on His children, but there were a few times that He allowed Satan to put afflictions on His children, as in the case of Job. This was to test Job's integrity with God, but God never allowed the affliction to remain, but turned it into a miracle to prove to Satan that Job was righteous, that he would remain true to Him under all circumstances, and that He (God) has the power to heal the afflictions of the devil;

in other words, that God had power and authority over the devil. Satan had accused Job before God and said that if God would take the hedge from about Job that Job would curse God to His face. God proved Satan to be a liar through the faithfulness of Job. Our faith in God and His Word will always prove Satan to be a liar. God does not afflict His children. I repeat—sin, sickness, and fear are tools of the devil, and God will not condescend to use Satan's tools. If you have been afflicted by the devil, perhaps it is because God has been bragging on you, but remember, you don't have to keep that affliction! God will turn it into a miracle right now by healing you, and your testimony can help others.

God wants your body to be strong so you can serve Him, so you can be a holy vessel through which His divine power can flow to help others. Get involved in a good, full-Gospel church. Get involved in studying God's Word and teaching it to friends and others. Give your life as a living sacrifice, holy and acceptable to do His service. Give of your money to the Lord to help promulgate the full Gospel (Good News) of the Lord Jesus Christ. Then, most of all, get filled and stay filled with God's Spirit as we are admonished to do in Ephesians 5:18 and 1 Corinthians 12:13. Take the Gospel of power and life and deliverance to the sick and the half dead. Be filled with the Holy Ghost as the Early Church was so that you will be empowered from on high to do God's work.

John the Baptist said, "I indeed baptize you with water but one mightier than I cometh, the latchet of whose shoes I am not worthy to unloose: he shall baptize you with the Holy Ghost and with fire" (Luke 3:16). And Jesus said, ". . . wait [tarry or seek] for the promise of the Father, which, saith he, ye have heard of me. For John truly baptized with water; but ye shall be baptized with the Holy Ghost not many days hence" (Acts 1:4, 5). Then Jesus gave the reason for such a mighty Baptism of His Holy Spirit, which was to follow John's baptism in water—the baptism of repentance. Jesus said, "But ye shall receive power, after that the Holy Ghost is come upon you: and ye shall be witnesses unto me both in Jerusalem, and in all Judea, and in Samaria, and unto the uttermost part of the earth" (verse 8). There it is in simple language. The purpose of the Holy Ghost is for you to *receive power* from God and *to be witnesses.* You will be very limited as to what you do for God's kingdom until you receive that power. It is available for every believer and for those who are willing to take time out to seek it.

Now back to the main theme of this chapter: you, too, can be healed of your diseases, regardless of how serious they are, and you can become a great witness for God just as this young, deformed Baptist friend of mine was. God can turn that curse into a blessing, but you must believe His Word and act upon it, just as this young man did. God works through faith and there is no other way on earth that He can work! He demands that we have faith in His Word if we are to get our prayers answered.

It is an insult to God for us to doubt His Word. You are healed because the Bible says so. No other reason or requisite is necessary because it is already written and it can never be changed. God provided it for you because He wants you to be well and happy. Tell the devil that you are believing God because "it is written." It is written the way that Mark 11:24 states it.

Repeat these words out loud: "I have what I prayed for and I prayed for a well body. I am already healed and I accept it in Jesus' name because it is written that way." Do this now, then Satan will have to leave you because he can't fight the Word; he can't stand before the Word. He can't defeat you so long as you are on the Word. Remember—stand on the Word because it is written that way and by God. Your faith in God's Word can heal you!

8

Read the Bible to Satan and Stay Healed

When I was invited to come to San Antonio, Texas, by the Reverend Odell Allen and his father to teach the Bible in a seminar on the subject of the Holy Ghost and the gifts of the Spirit, little did I know that I was going to witness the results of probably the greatest revival that America has ever known. I had churches all over that city open their doors to me to come and teach the Bible to their people.

One morning I was scheduled to teach in a church called Taylor Tabernacle. (It was here in this city that I was to learn of what happened in that great past revival, where there had been a great outpouring of God's Spirit, which no doubt changed the course of thousands of lives.) I was escorted to church by the Reverend Allen, and I felt led to teach on the subject of faith.

At the end of the service, a Baptist girl came forth and received the Baptism in the Holy Spirit. It was a glorious experience! When the service was over, we went to have lunch with the Reverend Taylor and his wife and they said to me, "We have been preaching the Gospel for over forty years and we have watched and heard how God uses you and we have great respect for your ministry. We want you to come back to our church and teach for a few days."

I went to that church on Easter Sunday and started there, teaching the Word of God. I remained there for four nights and taught, and then I went over to the other side of the city and taught ten nights.

Each morning they had me scheduled at a different church. Then I heard more fully the story of why the Spirit of the Lord was moving so freely and so beautifully upon the people who came forth to the altars to receive help from God.

The Reverend Mr. Taylor was over seventy years of age and he received the Baptism of the Holy Ghost under the ministry of the famous Rev. Smith Wigglesworth. The Reverend Mr. Taylor preached under a tent every day for one year in the year of 1928 in Canada. In 1929, God sent the Reverend Taylor to San Antonio, Texas. He rented an auditorium and started a revival under the direction of the Holy Spirit. He had three services per day, seven days a week, except Saturday, and he had two services on Saturday and a one-hour radio broadcast every night from 1929 to 1938 —a nine-year revival—three services a day for nine years.

Out of that revival came miracles of salvation and miracles of healing of all sorts: cripples got out of wheelchairs and began to walk; all manner of diseases were healed by God's mighty power; drunkards were saved and delivered from alcoholism and filled with the Holy Ghost and went out to witness and preach under

God's direction and anointing. The entire city and area around it was stirred for God.

As a result of this mighty revival, over fifty churches were build in San Antonio and surrounding areas. Between eight or ten churches are still operating today in that city and there are many churches in the different cities around Texas because of that mightly outpouring of God's power.

I was ministering on my second trip to San Antonio in the beautiful church called Taylor Tabernacle. I was speaking on Monday night to an audience in which there were many ministers present. These ministers came from various churches across the city. I used that familiar text, Mark 11:24, which you've read so much about in this book. In that meeting when I gave the altar call, immediately dozens of people flooded the front of the church to seek God.

One minister in the back of the church was so touched and moved by God that he began to scream out and push his way through the congregation under a supernatural power and he came and began to hug the pulpit, holding it as God's power melted him to the floor. He was completely overwhelmed by the mighty presence of God. (You see, when God begins to show you the lost world that is dying and going to hell, you begin to hear the screams and groans of the people in hell, and you begin to see people dying without God. It can so shake your natural understanding that all you want to do is to get on your face before God and scream out for mercy.)

The devil is so deceiving. He will constantly return and do everything within his power to get you to doubt

God's Word, to doubt God's call, and even try to convince you that heaven and hell are not real so as to dampen your vision and get you to relinquish your efforts in trying to win the lost and pray for the needs about you.

Out of that great congregation that night, and because the great outpouring of God's Spirit was so prevalent, people began to put their faith implicitly in the Scriptures which I had read from Mark 11:24 and began to act upon that Word. As a result, during the altar call about one-third of the people arose and came for prayer or for help.

The reason I am relating this incident to you is to show you that when the power of God begins to fall in a place, people's faith will begin to mount and rise up to the point where they can believe God for anything. When they see miracles take place right in front of their eyes, that enhances their faith even more, and those who have been slow and reluctant to believe will immediately get hungry for spiritual things and for freedom for their own spirits and bodies.

It is not necessary to have to witness such a manifestation of power as this to get an answer from God. Regardless of where you are, even if you are all alone, you can stand on God's Word as my deformed Baptist friend did and God will heal you. It is your faith and God's Word which healed you! You can continue enjoying freedom from the forces and power of Satan by reading God's Word to him. You must see that Satan hates the Bible because it is Truth and he can't stand the Truth of God.

Pardon me if I seem too redundant, but it is often

necessary to repeat again and again so that the message which I am trying to convey will sink in, but let me warn you again that Satan will try to prevent you from reading God's Word. He will keep you occupied on such seemingly legitimate things of life that he will crowd God's Word out; therefore, you must read it constantly, stand on it, act on it, and even read it out loud to the devil if he begins to try to bring doubt into your mind. It is your shield against his fiery darts (*see* Ephesians 6:16).

The power of God is released as faith of people begins to build. A girl set up a counseling appointment with me one afternoon. She had reached a point of desperation. She was a concert pianist, but she was letting her talents die and just wither away and she became miserable. She came to talk to me concerning the needs in her life and concerning her talent and the propositions which the world had offered her. As I was explaining that Jesus wanted and needed her talent to work for Him also, the mighty power of God came upon us and it began to surge through her and set her free.

Her mother was in a similar condition—a nervous wreck because of so many pressures. She was a staff secretary at a large air base and over the years job pressures became unbearable and she needed help. I prayed with her mother also and took authority over the thing which was causing those bad nerves and commanded them to leave her in Jesus' name. Jesus came to her rescue and the mighty power of God began to surge through her body also in a supernatural way. Her nervous system was healed and restored to normal and she told me that she was completely healed. She stated that she had been helped in some years past, but never on a permanent basis.

The reason that she had not received permanent relief through prayer was that she did not know how to fight against the devil and his forces. When I told her that she had to read the Bible to the devil to keep the victory, she did not understand what I meant. I said to her, "Oh, but this time it will be different; it is not going to come back and take you over again because I am going to teach you how to fight him, and the best way I know to fight him is to follow the instructions of James and rebuke him." (As has been mentioned before, James said in chapter 4, verse 7, to "Resist the devil, and he will flee from you.") I said to her, "That means to rebuke him in the name of the Lord and he will have to flee from you; that means don't yield yourself to your own understanding, to any kind of symptoms of pain or heartache. Resist them all in the name of Jesus and stand your ground. Jesus wants you to be free of pain. He wants you to be full of joy every day of your life."

She said to me, "What will happen to me when I go back to the office tomorrow and all of the pressure begins to fall on me as in times past? It has been years since I have felt like this and I don't want to lose this. Within a period of five minutes the power of God has changed me from a miserable, nervous wreck to a life that is filled with peace, joy, and understanding and the promise of a thrilling future."

I said, "Ma'am, I want you to take your Bible to work

with you; I want you to lay it on your desk and tomorrow, when Satan begins to come to you and tries to take you back to the life that you had yesterday, I want you to say, 'Mr. devil, I don't know if you can read or not, but just in case you can't, I am going to read the Bible to you and show you why I am completely healed, and why I will never be nervous again so long as I live, and prove to you that my life will be a life of peace, health, and beauty the rest of my life.' "

I continued, "Now you must read this out loud to the devil." I told her to say, "I want to read Mark 11:24 to you and you listen and you will find out why I am healed and why I am going to remain healed." I said, "I also want you to read the twenty-third verse of that chapter to him, which states, 'For verily I say unto you, That whosoever shall say unto this mountain, Be thou removed, and be thou cast into the sea; and shall not doubt in his heart, but shall believe that those things which he saith shall come to pass; he shall have whatsoever he saith.' " (That mountain may be a nervous condition, a spirit of fear, a physical handicap, a binding habit, a financial problem, or an incurable disease, but that mountain is simply nothing compared to the power of God, and by quoting this Scripture to the devil, he will have to turn loose his hold upon your life.)

As I continued my conversation with this lady I said, "Lady, you know that you have received that which you needed from God as you stood right here in this house. Is that right?"

She said, "Absolutely right. I am completely healed;

I am completely free. I haven't had a joy and peace like this in many years."

I said, "All right, now will you do as I tell you to do?"

She said "Yes, I will."

I said, "All right, then you read these Scriptures which I have just quoted to you. Read them out loud, sitting at your desk so that Satan can hear you." She promised to do it.

She came back to church the next night and gave a public testimony, telling of the marvelous way her life had been changed. She said, "I am not the same woman I was two days ago. I would advise you people to listen to God's Word and do the same as I did because I went to work today and took my Bible with me, and the pressure began to come upon me while holding two positions of high priority as it had in times past. Because of the confusion, the nervous condition began to try to return to my body. Then I picked up my Bible and said. 'Mr. devil, I am going to read you something.' " She turned to Mark 11:23 and began to read: "For verily I say unto you, That whosoever shall say unto this mountain, Be thou removed, and be thou cast into the sea; and shall not doubt in his heart, but shall believe that things which he saith shall come to pass; he shall have whatsoever he saith!"

Then she said "Mr. devil, I say that I am healed and I say that I will never be nervous again. Your tormenting days with me are over. My foundation is based on the promise of Jesus in Mark 11:24, also." She read that Scripture to the devil out loud. She said, "Now, 'what things soever' means my nervous system in this case, and as I prayed with Brother Hayes, we agreed and God's power set me free, and I desire to stay healed, so I will stay free and I have my healing now and forever!"

She declared that after she took that kind of stand against the devil orally, speaking as if she were talking to an individual, instantly Satan fled and the tormenting, confusing force began to leave in a matter of seconds, and she had no more trouble. But as a reminder to Satan, she spoke out loud again. "Now, Satan, I have received power in my body from God and by His help; you will never rob me of that peace and power again, because if you try, I will read my Bible to you again and you will have to flee because I believe what it says and I will stand on it now and forever!"

This family invited me to come to their home to have Sunday dinner with them. The mother and her husband, and the daughter and her husband, and other members of the family were present and it was obvious that these people's lives had been changed by the power of God because they took authority over the power of darkness which was coming against their minds and bodies, and even their homes. Not only they, but you, dear reader, have that same authority if you will just take it now in the name of Jesus Christ.

Jesus said that Satan, the enemy, had come to kill and destroy, but that He had come that we might have life, and that more abundantly (*see* John 10:10). We don't have to be beaten down or bullied by Satan's deceptive tactics, but we can have victory through quoting God's Word to him.

It is dangerous for us to build our faith on the doctrines and philosophies of men, for they are as sinking sand, but we must emphatically and implicitly build our faith on the Rock, Christ Jesus, and His entire Word. There is no other way to resist him but through God's Word. Don't ask him to leave you, your mind and body, and those of your loved ones whom he is afflicting, but quote the Word of God to him and command him to go!

Before Jesus began His earthly ministry, after He had fasted forty days and nights, Satan attacked Him at His weakest moment. He tempted Jesus in every manner that humanity can be tempted—on the pride of life, on the hunger of the flesh, on the lust of the eyes, but Jesus overcame him on each encounter by quoting the Word of God to the devil! He would say each time, "It is written," referring to the Old Testament. Read this account in Matthew 4:1-11. This is one of the greatest secrets in God's Word, and we are to overcome the enemy the same way. It is a revelation from God's Truth that we can overcome everywhere and every time in every situation and every circumstance!

We not only have the promises of the Old Testament as Jesus had, but now we also have the New Testament, which gives us even greater power and greater promises and authority through Jesus Christ, who came to fulfill the Law of God to its very last letter. Satan is still tempting and attacking, harassing and deceiving, and his emissaries (demon spirits) are being unleashed on the human race as never before. This battle will continue until Jesus returns and subdues him and confines him to his place of eternal punishment. In the meantime, we as believers must not panic or become despondent, but we must rise up and quote the Word to him and stand on God's promises until the battle of all ages reaches its final consummation.

In Revelation 12:11, the Apostle John states of the overcomers: "And they overcame him [that old dragon—the devil] by the blood of the Lamb [Jesus Christ] and by the word of their testimony. . . ." The blood is the shield and the Word is the sword that always defeats the enemy.

Satan is a defeated foe. He was defeated at Calvary. His works were defeated; his power was defeated; his authority was defeated. It was stripped from him and given to the Church—all truly born-again believers, who have accepted Jesus Christ as their Saviour and who are keeping His Commandments.

Accept the challenge! Rise up right now and believe God and praise God out loud for the victory over all the works of the devil. It is your prerogative—your divine privilege through the power, the blood, and the name of Jesus. Rise up and do it now. Your faith can heal you!

Books by Norvel Hayes

How To Live and Not Die

*The Winds of God
Bring Revival*

*God's Power Through
the Laying on of Hands*

The Blessing of Obedience

*Stand in the Gap
for Your Children*

*How To Get
Your Prayers Answered*

Holy Spirit Gifts Series

*Number One Way
To Fight the Devil*

*Why You Should
Speak In Tongues*

Prostitute Faith

*You Must Confess
Your Faith*

What To Do for Healing

*God's Medicine of Faith
— The Word*

*How To Triumph
Over Sickness*

*Financial Dominion —
How To Take Charge
of Your Finances*

The Healing Handbook

*Rescuing Souls
From Hell —
Handbook for
Effective Soulwinning*

How To Cast Out Devils

Power for Living

Radical Christianity

*Secrets to Keeping
Your Faith Strong*

*Putting Your Angels
To Work*

**Available from your local bookstore,
or by writing:**

Harrison House
P. O. Box 35035 • Tulsa, OK 74153

Norvel Hayes shares God's Word boldly and simply, with an enthusiasm that captures the heart of the hearer. He has learned through personal experience that God's Word can be effective in every area of life and that it will work for anyone who will believe it and apply it.

Norvel owns several businesses which function successfully despite the fact that he spends over half his time away from the office, ministering the Gospel throughout the country. His obedience to God and his willingness to share his faith have taken him to a variety of places. He ministers in churches, seminars, conventions, colleges, prisons — anywhere the Spirit of God leads.

For a complete list of tapes and books
by Norvel Hayes, write:
Norvel Hayes
P. O. Box 1379
Cleveland, TN 37311
Feel free to include your prayer requests and comments when you write.